Beneath A Sky Of Shared Stars

A Journey of Two Hearts

Abhilash L

BookLeaf
Publishing

India | USA | UK

Made with ❤ on the BookLeaf Publishing Platform
www.bookleafpub.in
www.bookleafpub.com

Dedication

"Beneath A Sky of Shared Stars" collection of heartfelt poems dedicated to the love of my life Jam.

Preface

"Beneath A Sky of Shared Stars" is a collection of romantic poems which captures emotions of love, admiration and devotion.
Each poem reflects personal experience, shared moments and the unique bond between two people.
It incorporates themes of romance, nostalgia and hope for future.

Acknowledgements

I would like to express my deepest gratitude to the love of my life, whose enduring support and inspiration have been the foundation of this romantic poetry book. This collection, born from the depths of my heart, is a tribute to the beauty and joy you bring into my life every day. Your belief in my words and feelings has fueled my creativity and given me the courage to share these pieces with the world.

Heartfelt thanks are also due to those who brought this book to life. Your encouragement has been invaluable, and your trust in my vision is deeply appreciated.

Finally, to all future readers, may these poems resonate with the love and passion with which they were crafted. I hope they bring moments of reflection and joy into your lives.

With all my love and affection

1. My sunshine

Most days arise with sunshine's gentle grace,
It stirs the soul, ignites the heart anew,
A dance of light that warms each cherished space,
Brings forth the joy in all that we pursue.

Yet once I dwelt in shadows, felt unsure,
When moments waned and dimmed my weary mind,
But then the monsoon came, a love so pure,
With you, dear heart, true solace I did find.

Each hour we share, a sparkle in the rain,
You are the light that banished all my fears,
In every drop, a promise to remain,
With laughter bright, we weave through all our years.

So here I stand, in gratitude I shine,
For you, my love, my everlasting sunshine.

2. You

My love, my dear, my heart's true guide,
My topmost wish, my constant pride.
Your beauty shines, a wondrous sight,
Your eyes, a star in darkest night.

Your smile, a sun, so warm and bright,
Dispelling shadows, pure delight.
With you, time flies, a fleeting grace,
Each moment shared, a sacred space.

To gods both old and newly born,
I pray our love, forever sworn.
May all our hopes and dreams take flight,
And bathe our days in purest light.

In you I trust, in you I believe,
My heart's devotion, I receive.
My love for you, forever true,
My dearest one, I'm lost in you

3. Week in review

As the lights dimmed and the final notes did fade,
I held your hand tight, in this moment's embrace.
With laughter and tears, together we've made,
A tapestry bright, none can ever replace.

Each whisper of joy, each shared, gentle sigh,
In the echo of dusk, our bond does ignite.
Let us capture this week, like stars in the sky,
For true connections bloom in the heart's warm light.

In the quiet of night, with memories clear,
We dance in the stillness, our spirits so free.
This friendship, a melody we'll always hold dear,
A song in our souls, forever to be.

4. Irrational fears of a rational mind

In realms where light and shadow gently play,
A dance of minds both young and wise unfolds,
The conscious guides, the youthful spirit sways,
In harmony, a tale of life retold.

We seek to shed the burdens of the past,
Embrace the joy that flickers in the night,
Through reason's lens and dreams that hold us fast,
Our hearts align, and chaos turns to light.

In flaws we find the beauty of our grace,
Each step a brushstroke on this canvas wide,
We journey forth, together we embrace,
A world imperfect, yet our hearts abide.

In balance found, we rise with spirits high,
A sacred dance beneath the endless sky.

5. Time

In this dance of hours, our souls intertwine,
Each second a whisper, your essence divine.
Moments stretch and bend, like twilight's embrace,
In the chaos of minutes, I find my true place.
So let the clocks tick, let the world spin around,
For in the garden of time, our love will be found.
Together we carve our own rhythm and rhyme,
In the heartbeat of forever, we'll conquer all time.

6. Missing you

I hold onto memories of those moments we've shared,
As distance may part us, my heart remains bared.
With each passing hour, I search for a sign,
Yearning for laughter, our souls to entwine.

Can this longing be whispered on soft, breezy nights?
Or painted in dreams where your laugh ignites lights?
I ponder the moments, the silence we break,
As stars weave our fate in delicate wake.

So here's to the future, to days bright and bold,
To stories unwritten and treasures untold.
For even apart, my love will still grow,
Like a river that rushes, a ceaseless flow.

7. Her

Her laughter is a melody, sweet and bright,
Illuminating shadows, turning day from night.
With open arms, she embraces the meek,
Her spirit a beacon, strong yet unique.
She's the heart of community, a radiant glow,
A garden of hope where empathy can grow.
She challenges the limits, breaks each mold,
Her story is daring, waiting to be told.
With each whispered dream, she ignites the fire,
Encouraging others to build and aspire.
So here's to her journey, ever bold and true,
The canvas of life, she colors anew.

8. Happiness

We share joy's bright light,
Elation's sweet delight.
Smile's a happy face,
Makes our hearts embrace.
Life's a gift so true,
In our hearts it lives anew.
Even sadness we may hide,
Never let your spirit slide.
Happy, we can be,
Appreciating you and me.
Pursue inner peace,
Peaceful bliss, release.
Peaceful joy we find,
In our hearts and mind.
You and I, together,
Embrace life's weather.
So let's smile today.

9. The wait

Like stars long for the dark to shine bright,
I'll hold your essence close, my guiding light.
Like rivers that long for the sea's embrace,
I'll journey through time just to find your grace.

With every heartbeat, my longing's refrain,
In silence, I whisper your name through the rain.
Though distance may stretch like the vast skies above,
I'll cherish the hope, for you are my love.

When shadows fall deep and the nights feel long,
I'll hum the soft notes of our timeless song.
For every heartbeat that yearns and waits,
Is filled with the promise of our intertwined fates.

In this dance of patience, my spirit will thrive,
For in each moment, I know love's alive.
As petals unfurl in the dawn's gentle light,
I'll be waiting, my dear, till we reunite.

10. Hypnotized

I'm feeling a sense of being hypnotized,
An old rubble needing fresh strokes of grace,
I soar like an eagle, but soon I'm denied,
Falling like raindrops, lost in the space.

This love and this hate, a dance in my soul,
A wish for the feeling to linger and stay,
To dodge the abyss, to keep myself whole,
With you as my sunshine, come brighten my way.

In shadows I tremble, yet seek your warm light,
With each tender moment our hearts intertwine,
In love's gentle embrace, we conquer the night,
Forever together, your hand clasped in mine.

11. Affection

I stand at the edge, where shadows meet light,
Questions unravel in the warmth of the night.
Each whispered promise a delicate thread,
Woven through dreams, where my heart dares to tread.

As the world outside dances in a gleaming embrace,
I find a sanctuary, a soft, sacred space.
With your love as my anchor, I finally see clear,
The treasures of connection that banish all fear.

No longer a ghost, merely a shell on the sand,
Together we blossom, hand in trembling hand.
In this dance of the heart, with rhythms so true,
I finally believe that I'm worthy of you.

12. Amazing day

We built our dreams like castles in the air,
With whispered secrets floating softly, light as prayer.
In the warmth of laughter, shadows lost their place,
Two souls intertwined, a delicate embrace.

With every sunset, we colored our fate,
In the rhythm of moments, we danced with fate.
Through storms and stillness, hand in hand we tread,
In this symphony of life, no words left unsaid.

As seasons change, and years unfold,
The stories of our journey will remain bold.
Forever etched in the fabric of time,
With you by my side, every day feels sublime.

13. Hope

We danced through shadows, whispered dreams in the
dark,
Embraced the silence, ignited each hidden spark.
With laughter that echoed like a sonnet's sweet rhyme,
Together we stitched moments, passing treasures
through time.

Your voice is my compass, guiding me through each
storm,
In the tapestry of life, you are the vibrant form.
Though chaos surrounds us, our bond will never fade,
For in the depths of our souls, a sanctuary was made.

So let's gather our wishes, cast them into the night,
With hope as our lantern, we'll set the world alight.
For every shared heartbeat, every tear that we spent,
Has woven a memory, a love that's heaven sent.

14. Magic

You came into my life like morning light,
A magic spell that whispered hope anew,
With every dream you helped me soar in flight,
Awakening the heart I thought I knew.

With you, each goal became a shining star,
An adventure waiting just to be claimed,
As laughter danced and dreams were never far,
My spirit soared, my heart no longer tamed.

This fleeting life, a canvas yet to fill,
With vibrant colors drawn from every scheme,
Together we will chase the truest thrill,
And paint our days with strokes of every dream.

So let us take this gift and run afar,
For in our hearts, we hold life's guiding star.

15. Paradise

This song is all about you,
Through storms and shadows you've fought true,
With every tear that found its way,
You held your dreams, come what may.

A life of trials, yet you stand proud,
Your heart a flame, your spirit loud,
In every hurdle, you found the light,
A vision of paradise, pure and bright.

Oh, what a place where hope takes flight,
A land of joy, where all feels right,
Your dreams like stars in a velvet sky,
Inspire my heart to also fly high.

So here's to you, with courage dear,
Your journey whispers, "There's nothing to fear,"
In your paradise, hope blooms anew,
This song, my love, is all about you.

16. Falling in love

In moments brief, your light transforms my soul,
Each heartbeat quickens, as defenses fall.
With fragile hope, I dare to take the toll,
For love may rise, yet risks the sharpest call.

I feel a spark, as if I am reborn,
Emotions whirl in colors bright and bold.
Though fear of hurt like shadows may be worn,
A chance for joy, a story yet untold.

I wonder if your heart aligns with mine,
If in this dance, you feel the pull and sway.
With every glance, a thread both bright and fine,
I dream of love that blossoms in the day.

So here I stand, with open heart and plea,
Just hoping you might also long for me.

17. All love

I stand in shadows, doubts begin to rise,
Will you accept the heart I freely give?
Through storms and calm, my love will never die,
In depths I've fallen, for you I must live.

Though time may part us, memories will stay,
I hope you smile when my thoughts cross your mind.
With every heartbeat, love never will sway,
For in your presence, my spirit's aligned.

You hold my essence, every joy and fear,
No matter the weather, I am all yours.
I wish you happiness, feel it sincere,
As I embrace love that endlessly pours.

Though I can't know what your heart may choose,
You've got all my love, in joy or blues.

18. My Home

In the stars I see your name, a celestial dance,
Guided by wishes, caught in a trance,
Each moment a spark, igniting the night,
With you by my side, everything feels right.

Through the shadows and dreams, let our story unfold,
A tapestry woven in threads of pure gold,
In this cosmic embrace, I vow to stay true,
For my heart found its home, and that home is with you.

With whispers of stardust and echoes of light,
We'll navigate time, our bond burning bright,
No matter the distance, no matter the trial,
With each beat of my heart, I'll cherish your smile.

So hold my hand tightly as we drift through the skies,
In this universe blooming, love never dies,
Together we'll wander through infinite space,
For in every heartbeat, I find your grace.

19. Me and You

Oh love, how deep my roots do grow,
In waters where the currents flow,
Like fish that leaps, yet cannot swim,
Or bird that yearns, yet feels so grim.

In chaos all around me swirls,
Your light, a hope that gently twirls,
In shadows cast, your truth shines bright,
A beacon in the shrouded night.

With every beat, my heart does claim,
In quiet whispers, calls your name,
For love is pure, it guides us through,
In tangled storms, it's me and you.

20. Love in Absurdity

In a world where laughter fades,
And meaning drifts like misty shades,
You declare life's dance a meaningless game,
Yet love, sweet love, ignites the flame.

A conscious choice, a daily vow,
To cherish hearts, to care somehow.
Though chaos reigns and fate may tease,
In love we find our truest ease.

Beyond the beauty, beyond the glance,
In every moment, a sacred chance,
To weave a bond that time can't sever,
In an absurd realm, love is forever.

21. Next to You

My heart beats only for your grace,
To be beside you, time and space.
No need for first place, I implore,
Just near you, ever, evermore.

Your triumphs bright, your sorrows deep,
With you I'll laugh, with you I'll weep.
Through foreign lands, our journey starts,
A bond of love, two beating hearts.

Your family, my own I'll make,
Your friends as mine, for goodness sake.
In sickness, health, through thick and thin,
Forever bound, where do we begin?

A part of you, that's all I crave,
No separate self, no distant wave.
Just intertwined, our spirits blend,
My dearest love, until the end.